Mythical Mischief:

An Adult Coloring Book of Supernatural Creatures

SAMANTHA KELLEY

Copyright © 2023 Samantha Kelley

All rights reserved.

ISBN: 9798386143237

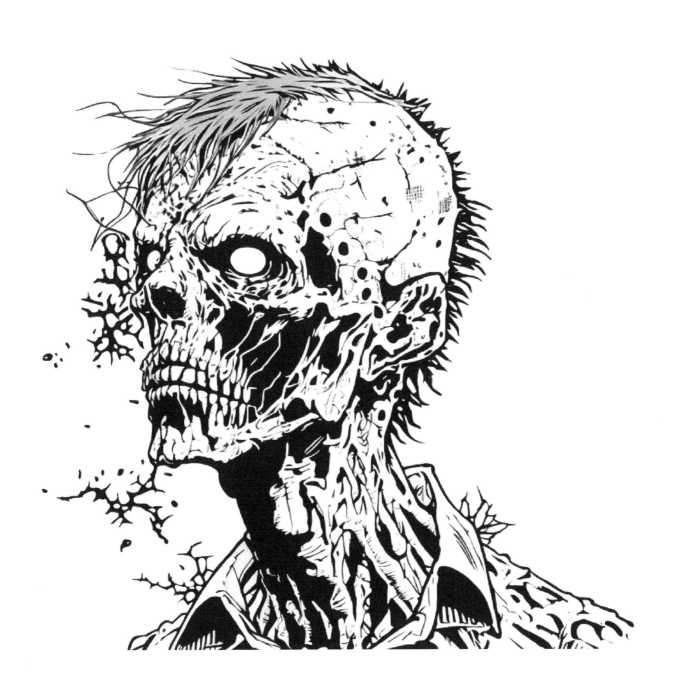

www.ingramcontent.com/pod-product-compliance
Lightning Source LLC
Chambersburg PA
CBHW082320161224
19130CB00057B/1233